TAKE TEN YEARS
1910s

MARGARET SHARMAN

Evans

EVANS BROTHERS LIMITED

Contents

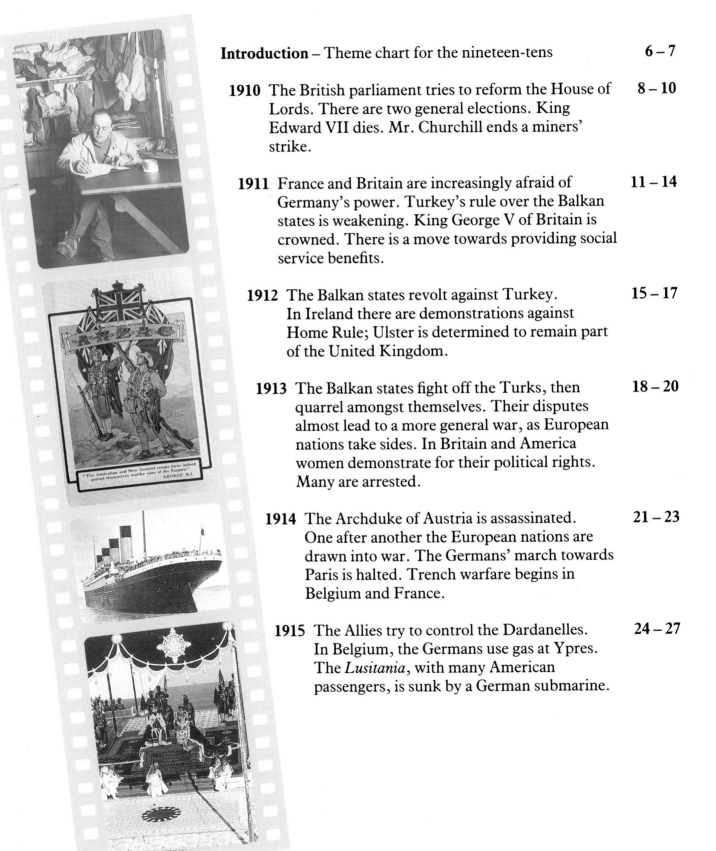

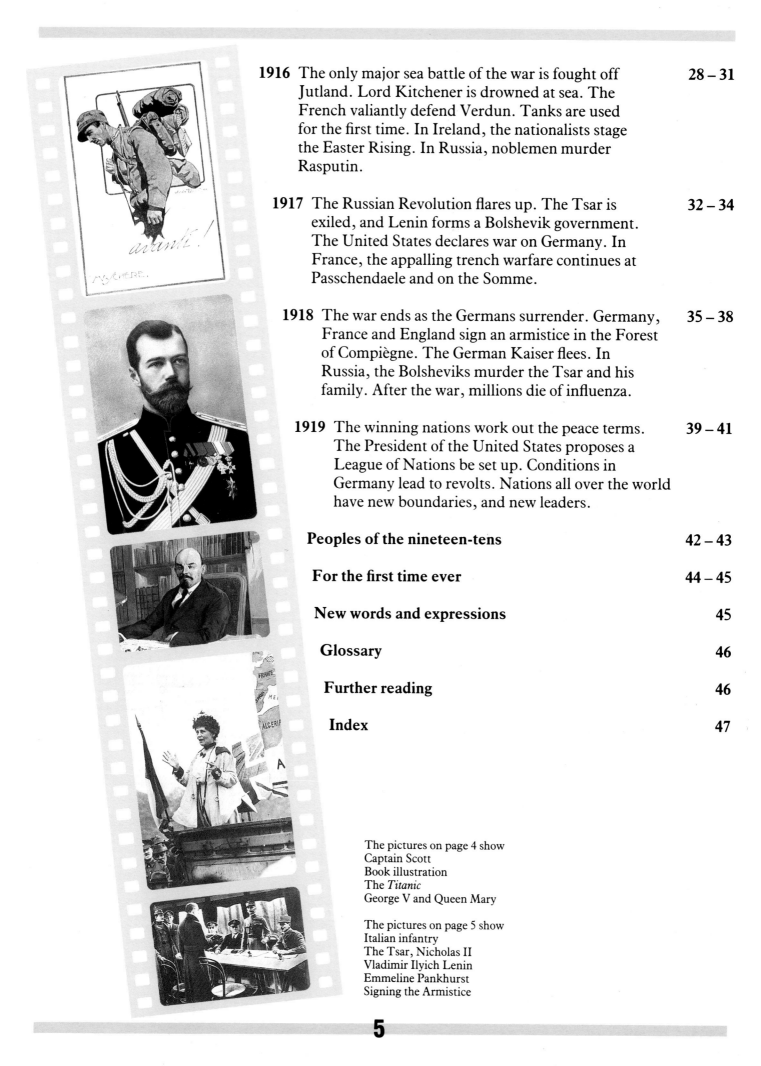

The pictures on page 4 show
Captain Scott
Book illustration
The *Titanic*
George V and Queen Mary

The pictures on page 5 show
Italian infantry
The Tsar, Nicholas II
Vladimir Ilyich Lenin
Emmeline Pankhurst
Signing the Armistice

Introduction

The 1910s saw the end of an old way of life in Europe. The Great War is the dividing line. Before the war, wealthy landowners all over Europe formed an upper class which was able to keep up a high standard of living. Their houses were run by servants, from the butler and housekeeper to the kitchenmaid. The sons of these wealthy families went to private schools (called public schools in England). Here they were taught a strict code of honour. They were to be their countries' leaders. They believed it was right to die for one's family and one's country.

These young men became the officers on both sides in the war. They led their men 'over the top' of the trenches, and were often the first to die. The men they led had joined up with great enthusiasm. They too believed in their country, right or wrong. On both sides, they suffered appalling hardships. Millions died in the mud of France and Belgium, and on the Russian front. Their graves are still honoured today. Those who survived no longer believed that war was 'glorious'. They went home believing that now things would be different.

Women in England and the United States had been protesting for some years against the lower status of women. Many joined the suffragettes, and fought for the right to vote. During the war they were able to do useful work outside their homes. Their self-respect and self-reliance grew as they nursed the wounded, and did the jobs of men fighting in France.

In America, nobody wanted to go to war. But when the Germans sank their ships they joined the Allies. America came out of the war with her lands intact and her economy in good shape. In Europe, and in the East, the survivors faced poverty and even starvation. Their towns were in ruins. The fight for the rights of ordinary men and women was beginning. In Germany, Italy and Russia, leaders who promised a better world were sure of a following.

YEARS	WORLD AFFAIRS
1910	Parliamentary crisis in Britain
1911	Germans land in Morocco Italians land in Tripoli, Libya
1912	Home Rule for Ireland debated Morocco becomes French protectorate Italians occupy Libya
1913	Suffragettes call for the vote in UK and USA
1914	The Great War begins, because of Balkan crisis
1915	The Great War Serbia defeated
1916	The Great War Americans invade Mexico
1917	The Great War Russian Revolution
1918	The Great War ends
1919	Peace Treaty signed Poland becomes independent

Introduction

WARS & CIVIL DISORDER	PEOPLE	EVENTS
	King Edward VII dies Crippin is hanged for murder Oldfield beats land speed record Kreisler, violinist, plays in London	Two general elections in Britain Miners' strike Halley's comet seen
	King George V crowned Emperor Pu Yi is deposed Marie Curie wins Nobel Prize	Strikes in Britain Unemployment benefits start Celebrations in India
First Balkan War	Wilson becomes US President Churchill is First Lord of the Admiralty	ANC formed in South Africa *Titanic* disaster Olympic Games in Stockholm
Second Balkan War Unrest in Ireland	Emily Davison, suffragette, killed by King's horse Isadora Duncan's children drowned	'Cat and Mouse' Bill Americans pay income tax
Battles at Mons, Ypres, Tannenburg, Falklands	Von Hindenburg leads German armies Pearl White is cinema favourite	Panama Canal opened Volcano erupts in Japan
Dardanelles campaign	Mustafa Kemal leads Turks at Dardanelles Anzacs win honour Nurse Edith Cavell is shot Rupert Brooke, poet, dies	Gas used in war for first time *Lusitania* is sunk Telephone message sent across Atlantic
Battles of Jutland, Verdun, the Somme Easter Rising in Ireland	Lord Kitchener drowns Shackleton reaches South Georgia Lawrence of Arabia leads Arabs Wilson re-elected US President Lloyd George is PM of Britain	Tanks used for first time Russian nobles kill Rasputin
Battles of Passchendaele, Caporetto	Lenin takes over in Moscow Balfour pledges help to the Jews Buffalo Bill dies	Hindenburg Line built America enters the war
Battle of the Marne	The 'Red Baron' is shot down Wilfred Owen, poet, killed	Armistice signed Russian Tsar executed Influenza epidemic Votes for women over 21 in Britain
Unrest in Germany	President Wilson asks for a League of Nations Dempsey becomes boxing champion Lady Astor is first woman MP	Massacre at Amritsar German fleet sunk at Scapa Flow

1910

PARLIAMENT IN TROUBLE
NEW LIBERAL BUDGET ROW

Feb 14, London A row is brewing between the British House of Commons and the House of Lords. Last year the House of Lords refused to pass the budget. Most of the Lords are Conservative voters. They tend to vote against Mr. Asquith's Liberal government, which is not very strong. The Conservatives have as many MPs in the House of Commons as do the Liberals.

KING'S SUDDEN DEATH

May 6, London Today King Edward VII died in London. There will now be no quick solution to the government's problem. If there were many more Liberal lords its difficulties would be solved. Mr. Asquith asked King Edward VII whether he would allow at least 200 Liberals to be made peers (lords). Only the monarch may create peers. The King was considering this request when he fell ill.

SECOND ELECTION THIS YEAR

Dec 20, London The British Prime Minister called for a General Election. But the result was almost the same as last time. There is a Liberal government, but with an equal number of Liberal and Conservative MPs. The Conservatives do not want more Liberals in the House of Lords. The situation is as it was at the beginning of the year.

WIRELESS MESSAGE REVEALS MURDERER

Oct 22, London Dr. Hawley Crippen's trial for murder ended today. The jury heard how he poisoned his wife in January, cut up her body and set fire to it. He hid the remains in his cellar and then disappeared, along with his secretary, Miss Edith Le Neve.

In July, police found Mrs. Crippen's body. By then the couple were on board a ship bound for Canada. The ship's captain was an observant man. He thought the police descriptions of Dr. Crippen and Miss Le Neve fitted two passengers calling themselves 'Mr. and Master Robinson'. He radioed the police by Morse code. This is the first time a wireless transmitter has been used to catch a criminal. The jury found Dr. Crippen guilty. He will be hanged next month.

Dr. Crippen and Miss Le Neve leave the SS *Montrose* under arrest.

German and British royalty attend the funeral of King Edward VII.

THE KING IS BURIED AT WINDSOR

May 21, Windsor Castle Flags in Britain were flying at half mast today for the funeral of King Edward VII. Seven European kings were at the ceremony. The German emperor, Kaiser Wilhelm II, accompanied the Queen. He was the late King's cousin. The King's eldest son has taken the oath as King George V and will be crowned next year.

THE HUNTING PRESIDENT IS HOME

June 19, New York Mr. Theodore ('Teddy') Roosevelt was given a big welcome here today. The ex-President has spent ten months hunting in British East Africa. His party shot over 10,000 animals. The African hunters called him Bwana Tumbo: Mr Big Stomach! Teddy bears are also stout; they are named after Teddy Roosevelt.

President Roosevelt enjoys picnicking with his family.

JOB CENTRES FOR UNEMPLOYED

Feb 1, London Mr. Lloyd George, the British Chancellor of the Exchequer, wants to "drive hunger from the hearths of the poor". It often takes months for an unemployed man or woman to find a job. The Chancellor's new Labour Exchanges should end the search for many. When they opened for the first time today, they were all crowded. There is no doubt about their popularity.

SOUTH AFRICA BECOMES A DOMINION

July 1, Pretoria The Union of South Africa became a Dominion today, becoming part of the British Commonwealth. The official languages are English and Afrikaans, a kind of Dutch. The government consists of British-born and Afrikaaner MPs, who are all Europeans. Africans are not allowed to stand for parliament.

PORTUGAL LOSES ITS KING

Oct 5, Lisbon Portugal was once a leading European nation. In the last hundred years it has been very unstable. Today there has been a coup against King Manoel. After bloody fighting in the capital he fled to Gibraltar. The army and navy, who led the coup, have proclaimed Portugal a republic.

RHONDDA VALLEY MINERS' STRIKE

Nov 14, Wales Coal miners picketed the mines last week. They have been told to work shorter (eight-hour) shifts. They are striking because shorter hours mean less pay. The Home Secretary, Mr. Winston Churchill, sent 250 unarmed London policemen to Wales. The miners fought them with iron bars and bricks. Mr. Churchill then sent armed soldiers to restore order. There is still much discontent in the pits, but the strike has ended.

NEWS IN BRIEF . . .

YOUNGSTERS PREPARE FOR ADVENTURE
Feb 6, New York and London Be Prepared to meet America's first Boy Scouts! A group of boys met today to form a troop like those which meet in Britain. Later this year, American girls will be able to join a similar troop – the Camp Fire Girls. In Britain they will be called Girl Guides.

A FASHION SENSATION
Sept, London Women of fashion no longer walk – they hobble! The new skirts are so tight at the ankle that walking is almost impossible. The Pope is shocked by the new fashion and has publicly condemned it. Most ladies wear the skirts with a hidden slit or pleat, so that it is easier to move.

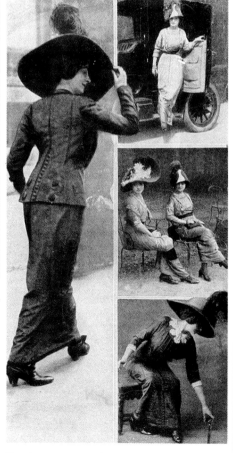
Reduced to a 'Chinese toddle' in hobble skirts.

VIOLINIST PLAYS A NEW CONCERTO
Nov 10, London Austrian violinist Fritz Kreisler today played Mr. Edward Elgar's new violin concerto with the Philharmonic Orchestra. The composer was conducting. Mr. Kreisler has played the violin since he was seven. He is one of the world's most brilliant musicians.

WATCH OUT FOR HALLEY'S COMET
May 20, London Halley's comet has reached a point 21 million kilometres (13 million miles) away. This is the nearest it will get to Earth. It can be seen at dusk when the sky is clear. In the United States some people think its tail lets out poisonous gases. They are buying 'comet pills' and boarding up their houses! Halley's comet returns to our skies every 75 years.

1911

THE SPIRIT OF UNREST
STRIKERS CLASH WITH POLICE AND TROOPS

Aug 17, London About 200,000 British railway workers are out on strike. Dockers in all the main ports have been striking for two months. Shop-keepers are running short of food supplies. In some towns, there is no electricity and no coal. In others, there has been serious rioting. Mr. Churchill has sent 50,000 troops to stop the riots. Armed soldiers are guarding the railway stations and signal boxes.

GOVERNMENT WELFARE SCHEMES WELCOMED

May 4, London Agricultural and industrial workers all over Europe have been rioting and striking for better pay and conditions. Many countries realize that they will have to provide social benefits.

In England, engineering and building workers earning less than £160 a year will now be entitled to sickness benefits. Each worker will pay 4d a week (out of a pay packet of about £3), the employer will pay 3d, and the state will pay 2d. In this way workers will be 'getting 9d for 4d'.

1d was one penny. There were 240 in £1.

Troops and police in armoured vehicles on strike duty in Liverpool

RECORD TEMPERATURES BRING TRAGEDY

Aug 30, London The strikes are over, but many strikers' families are starving. For once, the weather has been too good. On August 8 the temperature soared to 36.7°C. This is the highest temperature ever recorded in England. In the heatwave over 2000 children died.

INSURANCE FOR ALL

Dec 16, London All low-paid workers in Britain will now be insured. They can go to the doctor without payment. In the past, many people died of tuberculosis and other diseases because they could not afford treatment. Housemaids and manservants are afraid they will be sacked because domestic servants now get sickness benefits. Employers are grumbling that they can't afford their contributions. Already many are cutting down on their staff.

ENGLISH ROYAL EVENTS

THE KING IS CROWNED

June 22, London Today King George V and Queen Mary were crowned in Westminster Abbey. The Abbey was completely full. The congregation included lords, archbishops, members of parliament and representatives of the Empire. The ceremony followed very ancient coronation customs. Movie cameras filmed the scene outside the Abbey. They were not allowed inside. Next month the King's eldest son David will travel to Caernarfon Castle, where the Welsh people will welcome him as their new Prince of Wales. He is next in line to the throne.

The view from Buckingham Palace as the royal coach leaves for Westminster Abbey for King George V's coronation

CELEBRATIONS IN INDIA

Dec 12, Delhi King George has been crowned Emperor of India in front of a huge crowd. The princes of India were all there, in their splendid silk robes and jewelled turbans. The King announced that in future Delhi would be the capital of India, and not Calcutta.

King George V and Queen Mary in India

GERMANS LAND IN MOROCCO

July 2, Agadir The Germans have sent a gunboat to Agadir, in Morocco. The French are alarmed. Morocco has been under French protection since 1906. Germany has a large army and has become very powerful. The French and British fear that Germany may be a threat to world peace. They will hold talks with the Germans as soon as possible. Meanwhile the Austrians and the British are building up their navies.

LAST EMPEROR IS DEPOSED

Dec 29, Peking The Chinese people have ended the Manchu dynasty which ruled China for 260 years. The five-year-old Emperor, Pu Yi, has left his palace. Dr. Sun Yat-Sen, the revolutionary leader, has become the first President of the republic. He means to modernize China. For a start, he has forbidden men to wear pigtails. This hairstyle was introduced in the 17th century by the first emperor of the Manchu dynasty.

THE LORDS LOSE POWER

Aug 11, London The House of Lords has agreed to the Parliament Bill, which will restrict their power. The Lords may still vote against a government bill. But if they do, the Commons may debate it twice more. If they still vote for it, it will become law, even if the Lords oppose it.

ROYALISTS DEFEATED IN PORTUGAL

Oct 3, Lisbon There are still many people who want King Manoel back. Their makeshift army was finally defeated today by the republicans. The new government says all lords and dukes must now be called plain 'Mister'. Monks and nuns have been forced to leave Portugal, as the republicans are against the Church.

ITALY CAPTURES NORTH AFRICAN PORT

Nov 1, Tripoli, Libya Italian marines have landed at Tripoli in Libya, which is under Turkish rule. The Turks are neglecting their once-powerful empire. Italy has bombed towns and shelled ports. Countries in the Balkans are unhappy to be ruled by Turkey. They may seize the chance to rebel while Turkey and her empire is weak.

All pigtails must go, by order of the republic.

NEWS IN BRIEF . . .

CARS ARE EASIER TO START

Nov 1, Detroit, USA Louis Chevrolet, a Swiss-born car maker, is going to sell cheap cars. They will compete with Ford's Model T, and with General Motors' Cadillac. This car is being fitted with a self-starter. Owners will be able to turn the engine on by the flick of a switch. The present starting handles sometimes kick like a mule. Doctors say they will be glad to see the end of a common injury called 'starter's arm'!

MORE PEOPLE INHABIT THE WORLD

April 8, London The British population has risen by nearly 11 per cent in ten years. France's population has not changed. Russia has grown by a third to 160 million. The United States has welcomed thousands of immigrants, many from Eastern Europe who have come in search of work. The US population has grown from 76 to 92 million.

RAGTIME IS A WINNER

June 26, New York A million copies of 'Alexander's Ragtime Band' have been sold in America. Irving Berlin's tune is the greatest hit of all time. It is just right for the Turkey Trot. Critics say this new dance is 'disgusting' and 'indecent'. One young lady has even been jailed for dancing it. But with music like this, who can resist the temptation? Another Berlin hit is 'Everybody's Doin' it'. It was sung by the chorus of the Ziegfeld Follies' review, now in New York.

FRENCHWOMAN WINS AWARD

Dec 10, Paris Mme. Marie Curie has been awarded her second Nobel Prize. In spite of this great achievement, she cannot join the French Academy of Science, because she is a woman. Mme. Curie has extracted pure radium from a rock called pitchblende. You need about six tons of the rock to produce one gram of radium!

WHAT THE FASHIONABLE SET IS WEARING THIS SEASON

Autumn, London Dressmakers and milliners have done good business in this Coronation year. Hats are very tall and topped with feathers or even stuffed birds! Skirts are long and straight. Blouses have a V-shaped neckline. Most ladies have coats with fur collars, and carry fur muffs to match. Ladies driving the new motor-cars wear veils over their faces, and goggles over their eyes.

Gentlemen are equally handsomely dressed. They go to the City in tail coats, striped trousers and top hats. In the country they may wear tweed jackets and plusfours – trousers which reach the knee – and stockings. Their hats, gloves, suits, shirts and shoes are all made to measure.

1912

Jan 8	Black congress formed in South Africa
April 15	Sinking of *Titanic* on first voyage
July 1	Morocco given to the French
Oct 18	Italy wins Libya from Turkey
Nov 5	Woodrow Wilson elected US president

HOME RULE FOR IRELAND
ULSTER AGAINST HOME RULE

May 2, London The British government wants Ireland to rule itself. It has introduced a Home Rule Bill. If this bill is passed, Ireland will have its own parliament. Protestants living in Ulster – the Ulster Unionists – do not want Home Rule. They are afraid that an Irish government would consist of Catholics only. Most Ulster people are descendants of Scottish and English immigrants. They want to stay within the United Kingdom.

ULSTER UNIONISTS SIGN COVENANT

Oct 5, Belfast September 28 was 'Ulster Day'. On this day 200 Ulster Unionists followed their flag to Belfast's town hall. They signed a Covenant saying they would not recognize a Home Rule parliament. Many signed it in their blood. In towns and villages all over Ulster, over 237,000 men and 234,000 women have now signed the Covenant. They are determined to resist Irish independence at all costs.

NEW FRENCH PROTECTORATE PROCLAIMED

July 1, Morocco By a treaty signed in Fez, Morocco will in future be a French Protectorate. The Germans have been asked to leave. In exchange, they will get 154,000 sq.km of French territory in the Congo. No Moroccan or Congolese leader was invited to the talks which led to the treaty.

FIGHTING FOR THEIR RIGHTS

Jan 8, Pretoria Africans and liberal whites in South Africa have formed the South African Native National Congress. They are concerned about new laws which restrict African education, wages and land rights. The Congress hopes that the government will listen to the African point of view.

The South African Native National Congress later became the African National Congress.

The Covenant has forced the government to consider leaving Ulster out of Home Rule. But this is not the answer. Catholics as well as Protestants live in Ulster.

Ulster's Solemn League and Covenant.

Being convinced in our consciences that Home Rule would be disastrous to the material well-being of Ulster as well as of the whole of Ireland, subversive of our civil and religious freedom, destructive of our citizenship and perilous to the unity of the Empire, we, whose names are underwritten, men of Ulster, loyal subjects of His Gracious Majesty King George V., humbly relying on the God whom our fathers in days of stress and trial confidently trusted, do hereby pledge ourselves in solemn Covenant throughout this our time of threatened calamity to stand by one another in defending for ourselves and our children our cherished position of equal citizenship in the United Kingdom and in using all means which may be found necessary to defeat the present conspiracy to set up a Home Rule Parliament in Ireland. ¶ And in the event of such a Parliament being forced upon us we further solemnly and mutually pledge ourselves to refuse to recognise its authority. ¶ In sure confidence that God will defend the right we hereto subscribe our names. ¶ And further, we individually declare that we have not already signed this Covenant.

The above was signed by me at _____
"Ulster Day." Saturday, 28th September, 1912.

——— God Save the King. ———

WOMEN WANT VOTING EQUALITY

March 1, London This afternoon a group of women walked along three of London's smartest streets. Their hands were hidden in fur muffs. Then out of the muffs they pulled hammers and iron bars. The women smashed almost all the shop windows. They are suffragettes, who demand that women should be allowed to vote for MPs. Their leader, Mrs. Emmeline Pankhurst, drove to Downing Street and smashed the windows of No. 10, where the Prime Minister lives. She will go to prison.

Mrs. Pankhurst being arrested

WAR FLARES IN BALKANS

Nov 30, Sofia, Bulgaria Bulgaria, Romania, Serbia, Montenegro and Greece have formed the 'Balkan League'. The League is fighting Turkey and its dwindling empire. It has pushed the Turks out of provinces given them by treaty in the 19th century. The Turks governed these provinces very badly. For the first time aeroplanes are watching the movement of enemy troops.

DEMOCRAT ELECTED TO WHITE HOUSE

Nov 5, Washington The Democrats have won the presidential election. Mr. Woodrow Wilson succeeds Mr. William Taft as President of the United States. He said the country needs 'New Freedom' in politics, and a strong government. He is also concerned about individual rights and freedom.

HUNDREDS DROWN IN DISASTER

April 15, New York Towards midnight the liner *Titanic*, on her first voyage, hit an iceberg, which stripped the metal side from one end to the other. The passengers found there was not enough room on the lifeboats for them all. Over 1580 people drowned. The radio operator, who survived, wrote:

> "Smoke and sparks were rushing out of her funnel. There must have been an explosion, but we heard none. We only saw the big stream of sparks. The ship was turning gradually on her nose – like a duck that goes for a dive. I had only one thing in mind – to get away from the suction. The band was still playing. I guess all of them went·down . . . I swam with all my might. I suppose I was 150 feet away when the *Titanic* . . . began to settle – slowly."

AMERICAN INDIAN HERO OF OLYMPICS

July 22, Stockholm   A record number of competitors took part in the Olympic Games. The hero of the games is an American Indian named Jim Thorpe. He won both the pentathlon (5 events) and the decathlon (10 events). Although Thorpe claims he does no special training, he is undoubtedly the best all-round athlete in history.

For the first time, the games were accompanied by broadcast commentaries.

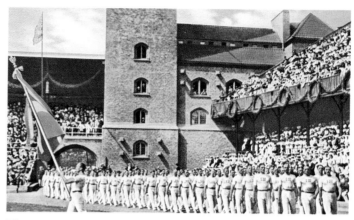

The opening ceremony of the Olympic Games.

Jim Thorpe, champion American runner.

THE ITALIANS ARE STAYING IN LIBYA

Oct 18, Tripoli   By a treaty signed today, Italy's occupation of Libya is legal. The Turks have given in. They are sending their troops to their Balkan provinces. Trouble is brewing for them there, too.

CHURCHILL TO MODERNIZE NAVY

July 22, London   Mr. Winston Churchill became First Lord of the Admiralty last October. He has asked the government for money to improve the fleet. He wants all warships' engines to run on oil, rather than coal. Mr. Churchill is alarmed at the strength of Germany's navy.

NEWS IN BRIEF . . .

TWO NEW STATES JOIN UNION

Feb 14, New York   Last month New Mexico was taken over by the United States as its 47th state. Today the state next to it, Arizona, has become the 48th state. They are both in the south of the country. Two more stars, representing the new states, will be added to the Union flag. There are 13 stripes on the American flag. They are a reminder that the Union originally had 13 states.

ICE IS NO SUBSTITUTE FOR WATER

Jan 9, New York   Shoppers today watched in horror as a skyscraper burnt to the ground. Firefighters had no water in their hoses. It was so cold that the fire engines were covered with ice. Pipes all over the city have frozen and most houses are without water.

NEW RUSSIAN NEWSPAPER

May 5, Moscow   A new newspaper, *Pravda*, is on sale in Russia. It is the official paper of the Bolshevik party, and is run by Josef Stalin. 'Pravda' means 'truth' in Russian.

CROPS AND CRICKET ARE A WASHOUT

Aug 31, London   This has been the wettest August in Britain since records began. Floods in East Anglia and the Midlands destroyed the ripening grain in the fields and ruined the harvest. In some places the record floodwater was nearly 1½ metres deep. Cricket fans have been disappointed. Several of the 'triangular' test match games, between England, Australia and South Africa, had to be cancelled because of the bad weather. Of those that were played, the result was: England 4; Australia 2; South Africa 0.

1913

TROUBLE IN THE BALKANS

YOUNG TURKS DISMISS TREATY

Jan 23, Constantinople The government has been overthrown by a political party called the Young Turks. They object to a treaty signed last month with the Balkan League. It stated that Turkey should give up her lands in Europe. The Young Turks want Turkey to keep Adrianople. To win it back, Turkey has attacked Bulgaria.

BALKANS STAGE A FREE-FOR-ALL

July 31, Bulgaria In May it was agreed that lands that were once Turkish should be divided between the members of the Balkan League. But they are quarrelling about how to divide them. First Bulgaria attacked the Serbs. While they were fighting, the Turks seized Adrianople. The Romanians have now invaded part of Bulgaria.

BALKANS HAVE NEW BOUNDARIES

Aug 10, Bucharest, Romania By a peace treaty signed today, the Balkan countries have agreed on how to divide the freed lands. Each country except Bulgaria has gained much territory. A new country, Albania, has been created. The Balkan quarrels almost led to a European war. Austria and Russia were ready to take opposite sides in the argument. The British Foreign Secretary has said, "We are sitting on gunpowder."

VOTES FOR WOMEN

SUFFRAGETTE KILLED BY KING'S HORSE

June 14, London Thousands of women have attended the funeral of Miss Emily Davison. She died after she threw herself in front of the King's horse at Epsom races. In prison she had often been forcibly fed. Once she piled furniture against her cell door. Prison officers turned a hose-pipe on her through the window, and she nearly drowned in icy water. The suffragettes are hailing her as their first martyr, and will always remember her bravery.

Miss Davison died in her protest.

AMERICANS ARE TO PAY TAXES

Feb 25, Washington For the first time since the Civil War, Americans will have to pay Income Tax. The United States government has to amend (change) the Constitution to make this legal. This is the 16th Amendment to the Constitution.

THE BRITISH GOVERNMENT PLAYS CAT AND MOUSE

March 31, London By a new Act of Parliament, suffragettes who go on hunger strike in prison will be temporarily released. They will no longer be forcibly fed through the nose, which is extremely painful. This practice was winning much sympathy for their cause. The suffragettes call this the 'Cat and Mouse' Act: the cat lets the mouse go a little, then pounces on its victim again.

MEN BREAK UP WOMEN'S PARADE

March 3, Washington Tomorrow Mr. Woodrow Wilson officially becomes President of the United States. Suffragettes hope he will help their cause. They have demonstrated outside the Senate House. The parade started quietly, but hooligans began to jeer at the women. In America, each state has to alter its laws to allow women to vote. So far, nine states have done so.

CROWD HONOURS FIVE BRAVE MEN

Feb 14, London Today a memorial service was held at St. Paul's Cathedral for Captain Robert Falcon Scott and his companions who died in the Antarctic. Last week a search party found their bodies. They were in a snow-covered tent 17 km (11 miles) from their supply base. Captain Scott's diary tells us what happened. When they reached the South Pole they saw the Norwegian flag flying there. Roald Amundsen's expedition had got there first. They were bitterly disappointed. On the way back the party encountered blinding snowstorms. They had very little food or fuel. They were too weak to reach their supplies.

Captain Scott and his team at the South Pole

PANKHURST SISTERS ESCAPE ARREST

July 18, London Miss Sylvia Pankhurst was almost re-arrested today. She spoke at a public meeting while on parole. Furious women fought the police to give her time to get away. Her sister, Miss Cristabel Pankhurst, is now leading the suffragettes from Paris, in order to avoid arrest. The suffragettes have many sympathizers. A notice in a shop window reads:

> Ladies, if we could give you the vote, we would. Please do not smash these windows. They are not insured.

DRIVE ENDS IN TRAGEDY

April 20, Paris Today two children with their governess were drowned in a tragic accident. Their car broke down on a hill. When the driver got out, it rolled back down the hill. It crossed a street and fell into a river. The children were a girl of seven and a boy of five. Their mother, Isadora Duncan, is a famous dancer.

IRISH QUESTION UNSOLVED

Dec 4, London The situation in Ireland is tense. The Home Rule Bill was passed by the House of Commons in January, but the Lords rejected it. They sympathize with the Ulster Unionists. A British officer commands the 50,000 men of the Ulster Volunteer Force. The Nationalists are recruiting for the Irish National Volunteers.

NEWS IN BRIEF . . .

STRAVINSKY'S BALLET IS HISSED

May 29, Paris Dancers performing Stravinsky's *Le Sacre du Printemps* for the first time could hardly hear the music. A large section of the audience booed and hissed it all the way through. They did not like Stravinsky's unusual music or Nijinsky's sensual dancing. The evening at the ballet ended in uproar.

FULL-LENGTH MOVIES ARE RELEASED

July 12, New York The French film *Queen Elizabeth* has had its first showing in the United States. It stars the actress Sarah Bernhardt. Earlier in the year a thrilling chariot race was seen in the Italian film *Quo Vadis?* Long movies like these are now being shown in special theatres called cinema halls.

NO CHANNEL TUNNEL YET

Aug 5, London The British government no longer plans to build a tunnel under the English Channel. The tunnel was going to cost £16 million. The government is afraid it would make England easy to invade.

DOWN WITH THE NUDE

March 30, Chicago Marcel Duchamp of France has caused a stir with his *Nude Descending a Staircase*. One critic called it 'an explosion in a pebble factory'. Others are asking which is the nude and which is the staircase.

TALL STOREYS REACH THE SKY

April 24, New York The new Woolworth Building was lit from top to bottom tonight. At 422 m (1384 ft.) tall and 55 storeys high, this is the world's tallest building.

LADIES' FASHIONS SHOCK AMERICA

Spring, New York Ladies of the smart set are shocking America by wearing Persian trousers. They complete the outfit with embroidered tunics and turbans. On their feet they wear oriental slippers. This strange fashion began when the French government allowed a lady archaeologist to wear trousers for her work in Persia. Nobody expected American ladies to copy her and start a new fashion.

AIR JOURNEY ENDS IN DISASTER

Oct 17, Berlin The world's largest airship, the zeppelin *L2*, has exploded in the worst zeppelin disaster to date. Twenty-seven passengers died. The *L2* flew for the first time only a month ago. The Kaiser once called its inventor, Count Zeppelin, "the greatest man of the century".

1914

MARCHING TO WAR
HEIR TO AUSTRIA IS SHOT

June 28, Sarajevo The Austrian Archduke Franz Ferdinand and his wife, the Duchess Sophie, have been shot dead. They were visiting the Bosnian town of Sarajevo. Bosnia, in the Balkans, is part of the Austrian Empire. This is seen as the latest attempt to free the Balkan countries from foreign rule. But the killer was a Serbian, not a Bosnian. His name was Gavrilo Princip.

Franz Ferdinand, Archduke of Austria, and the Duchess Sophie shortly before the assassination

SERBIA BLAMED FOR MURDER

Aug 4, London Princip has accidentally started a great war. Austria blamed the Serbians for the Archduke's murder, and has declared war on Serbia. Germany has sided with Austria. Three days ago Austria declared war on Russia, who is defending Serbia. France is supporting Russia. German troops are marching towards Paris through Belgium. Britain has a treaty with Belgium and today declared war on Germany.

The Allies	*The Central Powers*
Russia	Germany
France	Austria
Britain	Turkey
Belgium	
Serbia	

TROOPS ON A WESTERN FRONT

Aug 7, Southampton Crowds lined the streets today to watch the British Expeditionary Force (BEF) leave for France. They will march to Mons in Belgium, to stop the Germans reaching Paris. Everybody is certain the war will be won by Christmas.

Recruiting offices are being set up all over the country. This one is in Trafalgar Square, London. The poster reads 'Go! It's your duty, lad.'

21

THE BEF ARE 'CONTEMPTIBLE'

Aug 23, Belgian Front From a German report: Today we attacked British troops at Mons. They will not stop us reaching Paris. We have many more soldiers than they do. Our Kaiser has called the BEF 'a contemptible little army'. He assures us of victory before the autumn.

BOTH ARMIES MARCH SOUTH

Sept 2, France After fierce fighting at Mons, the BEF has withdrawn to the south. New boots, and the rough cobbled streets, caused many blistered and swollen feet. The men had very little rest or food. They marched 320 km (200 miles) in 13 days. The Royal Flying Corps is watching from the air as the Germans continue to march towards Paris.

THE WAR CHANGES DIRECTION

Oct 14, Ypres, Belgium Many of the German soldiers have been recalled to defend their eastern boundary. The Russians are marching towards it. The remaining German troops have been driven back across the River Marne, with heavy casualties. The Allied armies have now marched north to Ypres in Flanders. They are digging trenches for protection on the flat plain. The Germans cannot take Paris, but are trying to get to Calais. Whoever holds the coast will have a great advantage.

NO WINNERS IN TRENCHES

Nov 11, Ypres After nearly two months of fighting, both sides are exhausted. This trench warfare is quite new. One side shells the other's trenches; then their soldiers advance with rifles and fixed bayonets. The survivors fire on the advancing soldiers. Both sides use these tactics. The shells and the rifle-fire cause enormous casualties. British soldiers killed and wounded in three months amount to over 80,000; French casualties are 50,000. In England, over one million men between the ages of 18 and 30 have volunteered for the army. Women are being recruited as nurses.

GERMANY COUNTS ITS LOSSES

Nov 15, Ypres From a German report: It has begun to snow, and we are preparing for a cold and uncomfortable winter. We have 134,000 dead and wounded. Most of them were very young men, straight from school and university. The survivors are calling this 'the massacre of the innocents'.

BRITISH WIN FALKLANDS BATTLE

Dec 11, London The Royal Navy is celebrating today. Four German battleships have been sunk as they tried to capture the Falkland Islands. The British have coal supplies and a radio station at Port Stanley. The Germans did not know that there were two British battleships in the harbour. The battleships came out with guns blazing. Other Royal Navy ships are chasing the rest of the German fleet.

German and British soldiers meet on friendly terms on Christmas Day. British commanders have forbidden this fraternization to happen again.

CHRISTMAS IN THE TRENCHES

Dec 25, Ypres Over 2 million small brass boxes have arrived from England. They are Christmas presents for the troops and nurses. They contain tobacco or chocolate. This has been a day of goodwill: no guns were fired. Men of both sides walked into no man's land. They talked and smoked together. Tomorrow, the fighting will continue.

THE EASTERN FRONT

GERMANS WIN A VICTORY OVER RUSSIA

Aug 30, Tannenburg, East Prussia   General Samsonov has failed to invade Germany. The Russian general hoped to draw German troops away from France. The German 5th Army was badly outnumbered, but their troops are better trained. The Russian army contains many young recruits. The Battle of Tannenburg lasted just four days. The Germans, led by General von Hindenburg, took 120,000 prisoners. General Samsonov shot himself after the battle.

RUSSIANS BATTLE FOR POLAND

Nov 25, Poland   The Russians are fighting to keep the German army out of Poland. Four days ago they had the Germans surrounded. Suddenly the Germans cut through the Russian lines, taking 16,000 Russian prisoners. The war in the east is slowing down with sub-zero temperatures.

NEW PANAMA CANAL IS OPENED

Aug 15, Panama   The Panama Canal was officially opened today. Officials sailed the 64km (40 miles) through the canal from the Atlantic to the Pacific. Ships can now avoid stormy Cape Horn.

NEWS IN BRIEF . . .

IT TAKES TWO . . .

Spring, London   The latest dance craze, the tango, is taking hold of America and Europe. The Trocadero restaurant in London holds tango suppers. It is a dance of passion, to romantic Latin American music. Many parsons are speaking against it from the pulpit. In Germany it has been banned.

DAMSEL ALWAYS IN DISTRESS

April 4, Hollywood   Movie-goers love car chases, the rescue of ladies tied to railway lines and similar dramas. An exciting new movie series stars Pearl White, who trained in a circus. She does all the stunts herself. Her adventures will include aeroplane accidents, train wrecks and fires at sea. Each film will end with Pearl in danger. Movie-goers will have to wait for the next thrilling instalment.

20,000 HOMELESS IN JAPAN

Sept 30, South Kyushu   A volcano, Mount Sakurajima, has erupted in Kagoshima Bay. A cloud of lava and dust rose 9 km (5½ miles) into the air. The lava flow joined the mainland to a small island. Seven villages were destroyed.

CARS ARE BIG BUSINESS

Jan 5, Detroit   Mr. Ford's car factory was crowded out today. Police had to control hundreds of men applying for jobs. The reason for their eagerness is that Mr. Ford is doubling his workers' wages to a minimum of $5 a day. His business, and his wealth, have grown enormously.

Mr. Ford's cars are no longer built one by one. The parts are put together on an assembly line.

1915

THE GALLIPOLI CAMPAIGN

DARDANELLES CLOSED TO SHIPPING

Jan 1, London   The Russians have always reached the Aegean Sea and the Mediterranean through the narrow channel called the Dardanelles (see map). Now the Turks are not allowing any ships through. They are defending the Dardanelles with German Krupp guns. Russia is cut off from her Allies.

ALLIES ATTEMPT DARDANELLES BREAKTHROUGH

Mar 19, London   The Allies are trying to send ammunition to Russia to fend off attacks from Turkey. Yesterday a fleet of Allied battleships tried to sail through the Dardanelles. It was a complete disaster: the Turks fired on the fleet from both sides of the peninsula. A French battleship exploded, and two British battleships hit mines and sank. The surviving ships sailed back into the Aegean Sea. Russia is still cut off.

SOLDIERS FACE GAS HORROR

April 22, Ypres   In France the Germans are using a new weapon – chlorine gas. It rolled towards Allied lines today in a thick yellowish cloud. It burns the eyes, throat and lungs. Stretcher bearers are carrying victims to the Red Cross tents behind the lines. German troops advanced today wearing masks over their faces.

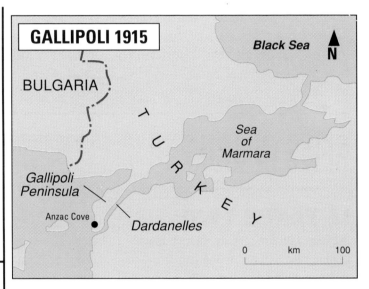

ALLIES LAND AT GALLIPOLI

April 25, London   Under Turkish fire, the Allies have landed men on the Gallipoli peninsula, at the entrance to the Dardanelles. The Turks were waiting in ambush as Allied troops landed on the beaches. Hundreds of men were killed. Hospital ships have taken the wounded to Egypt.

The country is rocky and bare. The survivors climbed great cliffs under fire, and then dug trenches for cover. There are too few men left to carry out a proper attack. They are of all nationalities. The British, French and Sikh troops have been under fire before. New to the war are the Anzacs (Australian and New Zealand Army Corps).

The Landing by George Lambert shows Anzac troops arriving at the Dardanelles.

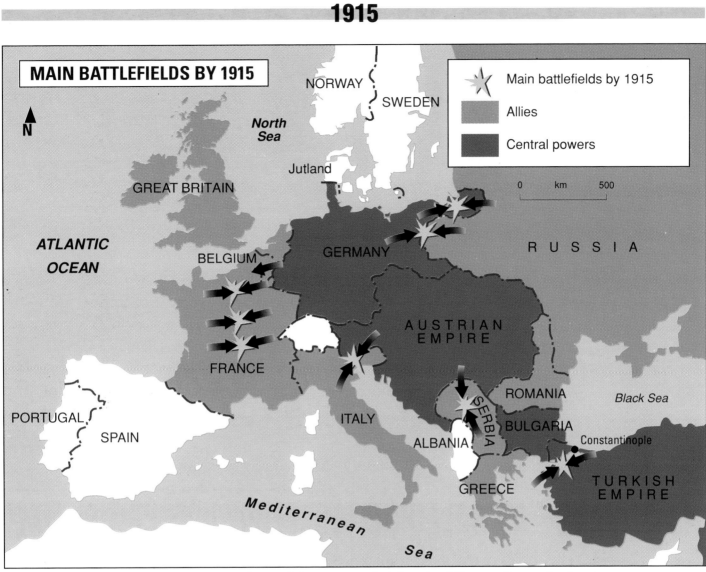

MAIN BATTLEFIELDS BY 1915

N

NORWAY

SWEDEN

North Sea

Jutland

GREAT BRITAIN

ATLANTIC OCEAN

BELGIUM

GERMANY

R U S S I A

A U S T R I A N E M P I R E

FRANCE

PORTUGAL

SPAIN

ITALY

SERBIA

ROMANIA

Black Sea

BULGARIA

Constantinople

ALBANIA

GREECE

T U R K I S H E M P I R E

Mediterranean Sea

★ Main battlefields by 1915

Allies

Central powers

0   km   500

In this the second year of the war, the Central Powers are fighting the Allies on five major fronts.

French soldiers in their trenches

Turkish guns at Gallipoli

British troop positions at Anzac Cove

NO ADVANCE AT GALLIPOLI

June 25, London   The Allies have landed more troops at Gallipoli. It is intensely hot, water is short, and many men have died of dysentery. The fighting goes on day and night. The Anzacs are particularly daring, but every time they attack, fierce Turkish fire holds them back. The Turkish force, led by Mustafa Kemal, is small but courageous. The Turks are determined not to surrender the peninsula. If they did, the Allies could take the Turkish capital, Constantinople.

TORPEDO SINKS BRITISH LINER

May 8, London   The largest passenger ship in the world, the *Lusitania*, has been torpedoed by a German submarine, or U-boat. U-boats have sunk hundreds of merchant ships. The Germans are trying to stop food reaching Britain. But this attack on an unarmed ship has shocked everyone. Over 100 Americans were among the 1200 people drowned. President Wilson is going to protest to Germany. People are wondering how long he can keep the United States out of the war.

TROOPS LEAVE GALLIPOLI

Dec 31, London   The Germans are sending troops to help the Turks. The Allies cannot hope to win now. By night, and in bitterly cold weather, Allied soldiers are quietly boarding troop ships. They are leaving their stores behind. The retreat will go on into the New Year. The campaign has left 30,000 dead and 74,000 wounded. Nothing has been won, only the fame of valiant men. The Anzacs' bravery will never be forgotten.

SOME GERMAN PLANS REVEALED

July 24, New York   Although the United States and Germany are not at war, German secret agents are spying in America. A US secret service man followed a suspect, and snatched his briefcase. It contained plans to wreck American ships and factories. The Germans had also arranged for cinemas to show pro-German films, and newspapers to carry pro-German articles. Two German officials have been told to leave the United States.

NURSE SHOT IN BELGIUM

Oct 12, Brussels Miss Edith Cavell, a British nurse, was shot by the Germans this morning. She ran the Brussels School of Nursing. She nursed any wounded soldier, whatever his nationality. The Germans discovered that she also helped British soldiers to escape. They executed her for treason.

SERBIA IS DEFEATED

Dec 21, Serbia The Germans now occupy the whole of Poland. The Bulgarians have joined with the Germans and captured Serbia. Hundreds of starving Serbians are escaping to Albania.

Nurse Edith Cavell at home

NEWS IN BRIEF . . .

MOVIE THREATENS RACE TENSION

Feb 8, Los Angeles An epic film, *The Birth of a Nation*, is seen as America's answer to the successful Italian film *Quo Vadis?* But black leaders have protested. The film shows the early history of the racist Ku Klux Klan. They are afraid it may lead to a Klan revival, and anti-black feeling.

INDIAN LAWYER SIDES WITH POOR

Nov 22, Bombay An Indian lawyer, Mr. Mohandas Gandhi, has returned home from South Africa. During his 20 years in South Africa he encouraged Africans to resist unjust laws, but without violence. Mr. Gandhi led demonstrations, and wrote newspaper articles. He went to prison for his beliefs. The Prime Minister of South Africa, General Jan Smuts, respected his ideals. Mr. Gandhi has become a hero to Indian nationalists.

BUDGET INCREASES INCOME TAX

Sept 21, London High taxes were announced today. Income tax for those earning more than £130 a year will be just under 3s in the pound. There will be import duties of 33 per cent on luxury items so that imports will be reduced. Ships can then be used to carry food and war supplies.

TELEPHONE CALL ACROSS THE ATLANTIC

Oct 21, Washington In January, Alexander Bell, inventor of the telephone, phoned right across the American continent. Today a message was sent from the eastern United States across the Atlantic Ocean to Paris.

FASHION NEWS

Spring, London Ladies' hats are smaller this year. They have broad, deep crowns and wide brims. Skirts are worn just above the ankle, to show leather shoes or ankle boots with 5 cm (2 inch) heels. Men's boots are often covered with cloth spats.

A POET DIES AT SEA

April 23, Greece Mr. Rupert Brooke, the poet, died today of blood poisoning. He was 27. He was an officer on a ship sailing for the Dardanelles. His most famous poem 'The Soldier' begins:

If I should die, think only this of me:
That there's some corner of a foreign field
That is for ever England . . .

That 'corner' will be on the Greek island of Skyros.

1916

THE WAR AT SEA

U-BOATS SINK NEUTRAL SHIPS

April 18, Washington German U-boats continue to sink ships belonging to countries that are not at war. Some of these ships are American. After the sinking of the *Lusitania* last year, the German government apologized to the United States. President Wilson has protested to the Germans again. By international agreement, neutral ships should be left alone.

WARSHIPS FIGHT FIERCEST BATTLE

June 1, London Yesterday 259 warships and 100,000 men fought a bloody battle in the North Sea off Jutland. The British and German fleets bombarded each other with shells, torpedoes and guns. Many ships blew up and sank. Hundreds of sailors were killed. Neither side really won the battle. The fleets sailed home, exhausted, during the night. This is the biggest sea battle of the war.

WOMEN DOING TOUGH WAR WORK

Feb 13, London There have never been so many opportunities for women. The government is going to employ 400,000 women in a new Land Army and Forestry Corps. About 80,000 women have joined the Voluntary Aid Detachment (VAD). They work in hospitals and drive ambulances. After the war is over, will they want to stay at home?

NEWS FROM THE BATTLEFIELDS

'THEY SHALL NOT PASS,' SAY FRENCH

June 24, Verdun, France The French have been bombarded with more than 2 million German shells. The Germans are trying to capture the steel-and-concrete fortresses that ring the town of Verdun. They are using flame-throwers and gas shells. These are more accurate and deadly than the gas canisters that were used at Ypres. The casualties are appalling.

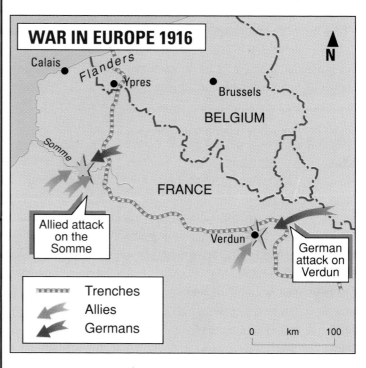

Major battles this year are being fought between enemy trenches in Belgium and France.

WAR MINISTER IS DEAD

June 5, London The British Secretary for War, Lord Kitchener, decided to go to Russia by sea to talk with the Tsar about new battle plans. Lord Kitchener was drowned when the cruiser he was sailing in hit a mine and sank. Everyone in England knows Lord Kitchener's recruiting poster. It persuaded three million men to volunteer for the Western Front. Mr. Lloyd George will succeed Lord Kitchener at the War Ministry.

BRITONS

"WANTS" YOU

JOIN YOUR COUNTRY'S ARMY!

GOD SAVE THE KING

Reproduced by permission of LONDON OPINION

THE BRITISH ADVANCE IN TANKS

Sept 15, France The Allies have a new weapon! Today 18 armoured tanks crossed the boggy craters and fallen trees of no man's land. They fired on German positions from close range. The crews report that the tanks are dreadfully noisy and stiflingly hot. But they may change the way the war is fought. Mr. Lloyd George criticizes the generals for using tactics which result in the deaths of so many men.

RUSSIAN SURPRISE ATTACK SUCCEEDS

Sept 15, Lvov On June 4 the birthday party of the Austrian Archduke was interrupted by a surprise Russian attack. The Russians advanced rapidly, and now occupy 100 km (62 miles) of enemy territory. They have taken about 400,000 Austrian prisoners and captured guns and ammunition.

A SECOND BATTLE ON THE SOMME

July 1, France Today has been the worst single day in history for casualties. The British bombarded the Germans on a front 28 km (17 miles) long. They hoped to relieve pressure on the French at Verdun. The Germans survived the bombardment in deep trenches. At Verdun and on the Somme, nearly 2 million men died.

IRISH NATIONALS REVOLT IN EASTER RISING

May 12, Dublin Troops have had to be recalled from France to go to Ireland. Two weeks ago a thousand Irish Nationalists seized the Dublin post office and the Court House. They proclaimed an Irish republic. After a fierce battle, British troops restored order. The leaders of the rising were captured and have been shot.

GREAT EXPLORER IS RESCUED

Aug 30, London Two years ago Mr. Ernest Shackleton set out with a team of explorers to cross Antarctica. His ship, *Endurance*, was caught in pack-ice in January 1915. For nine months it drifted helplessly. At last the party managed to reach a deserted island. In order to fetch help for his exhausted men, Mr. Shackleton sailed alone in a small open boat for 1300 km (800 miles) to South Georgia. He reached a whaling station which had a wireless transmitter. A relief expedition has now picked up all the men.

Ernest Shackleton in arctic gear

'HOLY' RASPUTIN IS DEAD

Dec 30, St. Petersburg Two Russian noblemen have murdered the extraordinary Gregori Rasputin. Ten years ago this man treated the only son of the Tsar and Tsarina of Russia, who has haemophilia. Rasputin became the adviser of the Tsarina, and through her, of the Tsar himself. But he was not the holy man the Tsarina thought him. Russians believed his influence was evil. Rasputin survived poison, so his murderers shot him. Still alive, he was thrown into a river where he drowned.

UNDER NEW LEADERSHIP

Dec 7, Washington Last month Mr. Woodrow Wilson was re-elected President of the United States. He is popular because people say he kept the Americans out of the war: but for how long can he do so? In Britain Mr. Asquith has resigned as prime minister. His successor is Mr. David Lloyd George, who is determined to fight the war to a speedy finish.

A VIEW FROM THE TRENCHES

France "If only the people of England could have seen what I saw yesterday they would not grumble about air raids. I saw motor lorries sunk in the mud over the wheels, also horses with just part of their heads showing above the swamp, also 2 tanks which were in the Push and were buried – the men who were still in them will never be able to tell the tale of the fight but they were heroes.

. . .There are men now in the trenches full of water who are nearly dead, they are fast dying of cold, they go sick, see the doctor, go back and try to stick it until they get relieved. . ."

(Daniel Sweeney, a soldier, from *Greater Love*, ed. M. Moynihan, W. H. Allen 1980)

The four allied leaders. Woodrow Wilson is on the right.

AMERICAN TROOPS ENTER MEXICO

June 21, Mexico   American troops have crossed the border into Mexico. They are searching for a rebel named Pancho Villa. He has led raids across the Mexican border into North America. In January his soldiers stripped and shot 18 American miners. Similar incidents followed. The Americans are taking tough action to protect their citizens. They fear that a full-scale war may break out between the two countries.

The outlaw Pancho Villa and his men

NEWS IN BRIEF . . .

BRITISH SUMMER TIME ARRIVES
May 21, London   Today all clocks in the country were put forward by one hour. This new move will give everyone more daylight working hours. Most people welcome lighter evenings. British Summer Time ends in October.

SERBS SALUTE EXTRAORDINARY WOMAN
Nov 30, Belgrade   Flora Sandes was nursing in Serbia when the army fled into Albania last December. She dressed as a man and joined the army. She was seriously wounded fighting the Turks. The Serbs have given her a medal for bravery.

VICTORIA CROSS FOR YOUNG HERO OF BATTLE OF JUTLAND
July 6, London   Jack Cornwall was posthumously awarded the VC today. Six weeks ago he died at the Battle of Jutland. He was only 16. Jack was one of the gun crew on HMS *Chester* when the ship was attacked by four German ships. Within a few minutes his mates on the gun turret were dead. Jack stuck to his post and continued firing until he too was killed.

MOVIES MAKE MONEY
Oct 31, Hollywood   Six years ago Hollywood was a quiet country town surrounded by lemon groves. Now 52 film companies have their headquarters here. The cinema has become the fifth largest American industry. Charlie Chaplin has made 34 films – in 34 weeks. He earns more than does the President of the United States. The country's film star sweetheart, Mary Pickford, earns a million dollars a year.

Film star Mary Pickford

1917

REVOLUTION IN RUSSIA
MORALE LOW FOR ARMY AND CIVILIANS

January, Petrograd   The Tsars of Russia rule over a huge country where life is harsh for most people. Rich noble families live in splendid houses while those who work for them live in dreadful poverty. To add to their discontent, the Russian people are sick of the war. They have asked the government to make peace with Germany. The army is short of ammunition and warm clothing. Soldiers are deserting from the Russian front. The Tsar, Nicholas II, is in charge of the army. People blame him for the deaths of two million men in battle.

TSAR DEPOSED BY GENERALS

March 15, Petrograd   The army generals told the Tsar that he must give up his throne. He has done nothing about the food shortages and general unrest. Starving people are rioting all over the country. Factory workers are on strike. The railway system has broken down. The temperature is below zero, and there is little firewood or coal.

BOLSHEVIKS SEIZE THEIR CHANCE

April 20, Petrograd   Vladimir Lenin, leader of the Bolshevik (socialist) party, wants to replace the weak government. He has called for an end to the unpopular war; and he wants to nationalize industry.

RED REVOLUTION SUCCEEDS

Nov 7, Petrograd   Lenin's Red Guards seized the Winter Palace today. This is where the government has its offices. The Guards locked the government ministers in the palace cellars. Lenin is ready to form his own government. He has achieved the first of his aims.

LENIN'S REFORMS BEGIN

Dec 5, Brest-Litovsk   The new Bolshevik government has signed an armistice with Germany. For the Russians, the war is over. Lenin wants factories to be controlled by workers' councils (soviets). The government will take over farms belonging to the Church, to landlords and rich farmers. Lenin's slogan is 'Peace, freedom and bread'.

A portrait of Lenin, the Bolshevik leader

NEWS FROM THE WAR ZONES

ALLIES FACE HINDENBURG LINE

March 30, Flanders From a German report: Our armies have been digging fortified trenches behind the front line, from Arras to Soissons. This Hindenburg Line is about 50 km (31 miles) long. It has concrete dugouts, and is served by railways which bring in supplies. In front are many fences of barbed wire. No Allied troops will be able to cross it.

AMERICA DECLARES WAR

April 6, Washington President Wilson's government has declared war on the Germans. In a speech to Congress the President said "The world must be made safe for democracy." The Allies are overjoyed at the news.

MUD AND RAIN ADD TO MISERY

August 30, France Today, near the village of Passchendaele, one of the worst battles of the war is being fought. It rains all the time. Soldiers fight ankle-deep in thick mud. Mules and wounded men drown in shell-holes. The hail of bullets and shells never stops. Nobody who survives this battle will ever forget Passchendaele.

THE YANKS ARE ENTHUSIASTIC

June 5, Washington Recruiting offices were open for 12 hours today. The response was incredible. Nearly 10 million men have joined the US army. Recruiting posters all over the country show Uncle Sam (a nickname for the USA) saying "I want YOU for the U.S. Army". The new theme song is 'Over There' – 'there' being the Western Front.

Recruiting posters like this one encouraged Americans to join the war.

ITALIANS FLEE AUSTRIAN ADVANCE

Nov 9, north-east Italy The Italians joined the Allies two years ago. They have been fighting the Austrians with some success. But today they were defeated at Caporetto. They have lost a huge area to the German and Austrian armies. Thousands were killed. Italian survivors had to leave their weapons behind as they retreated. Peace in Europe seems to be as far away as ever.

PLANES BOMB LONDON

June 14, London German planes made a daylight bombing raid yesterday. A bomb fell on a school, killing many children. Another hit a train. In the past, zeppelins have been used as bombers. Planes are faster, and not so easy to hit as the airships.

JEWS DELIGHTED BY BALFOUR'S DECLARATION

Nov 8, London Mr. Arthur Balfour, the British Foreign Secretary, has declared support for a Jewish national home in Palestine. The Jews are scattered all over the world. Many hope they will have their own homeland at last.

ENGLAND FACES FOOD SHORTAGES

March 20, London There is only about a month's supply of wheat in the country. There is a shortage of other foods as well. The shortages are caused by the U-boats, German torpedo-carrying submarines, which sink a quarter of all the ships coming into British ports. This month the Germans have sunk 134 neutral ships as well.

WOMEN URGED TO JOIN FORCES

Nov 29, Admiralty, London The Admiralty is going to recruit women into the navy. They will be called the Women's Royal Naval Service (WRNS). Members of the Women's Army Auxiliary Corps (WAAC) are already in France. They work just behind the front lines, in the kitchens, the store rooms, and the offices.

NEWS IN BRIEF . . .

RED CROSS IS HONOURED

Dec 10, Stockholm The International Red Cross, based in Geneva, has won this year's Nobel Peace Prize. Red Cross volunteers are working in appalling conditions on the battle fronts. Thousands of soldiers owe their lives to the gallant Red Cross.

OLD CONTEMPTIBLES REMEMBERED

Aug 25, London A new decoration, the Mons Star, will be given to all those who fought at Mons and Ypres in 1914. They will be known as the 'Old Contemptibles'. (The Kaiser called them 'a contemptible little army'.)

Another medal was awarded for the first time today. It is for civilians who have served Britain and the Empire well. It is called the Order of the British Empire (OBE).

END OF A LEGEND

Jan 10, Denver, USA Buffalo Bill, whose real name was William Cody, died today. As a young man he was an army scout during wars against the Indians in the 'Wild West'. Many legends grew up about his courage and daring, and the thousands of buffaloes he had shot. In 1883 he started a Wild West Show, which toured the United States. One of his star performers was a young woman called Annie Oakley, who was a crack shot. She once shot the ash off a cigarette in the mouth of the Kaiser! The Wild West Show lasted for 30 years. Everyone wanted to see Buffalo Bill.

FROM TSAR TO STAR?

March, Hollywood Mr. Lewis J. Selznick, the film producer, has invited ex-Tsar Nicholas to act in movies. Mr. Selznick is an immigrant from Russia. The ex-Tsar is not likely to accept this strange invitation.

JUDGE SAYS NO TO BIRTH CONTROL

Sept 30, New York Miss Margaret Sanger has been sentenced to jail. She opened a birth control clinic last year. The judge said birth control was against the law of the state, and also the law of God.

Margaret Sanger, pioneer of birth control

1918

VICTORY FOLLOWS DEFEAT
GERMANS PUSH THE ALLIES BACK

April 10, River Marne, France The year has started badly for the Allies. A week ago, a million German soldiers left the Hindenburg Line and advanced toward the River Marne. They bombarded Allied trenches for five hours, with 6,000 guns and with gas shells. Their new super-gun, nicknamed 'Big Bertha', fired on Paris from 100 km (62 miles) away. For 16 days the whole Allied army had to retreat as the Germans pressed forward.

GERMANS LOSE ACE PILOT

April 21, France Everybody on the Somme has heard of the 'Red Baron'. This German airman flew in his red plane with great skill and daring. Now he has been shot down and killed. Allied soldiers took souvenirs from the plane, and formed a guard of honour at his funeral. Although thousands of airmen on both sides have been killed in this war, they felt that the Red Baron was special.

Baron Manfred von Richthofen – the 'Red Baron'

Woodrow Wilson has been re-elected as President of the USA. Americans support his decision to enter the war in support of the Allies.

ALLIES SUDDENLY GAIN GROUND

Aug 8, Amiens The big offensive in April exhausted German troops. Away from the Hindenburg Line they are not so well protected; they are short of food and medical supplies. The Allies have sent in 450 tanks to batter the German gun positions, and the Flying Corps is bombing the trenches. Thousands of American soldiers are arriving each month in good health and eager to fight. Hundreds of Germans are surrendering every day.

The French and British advance near Amiens.

TURKS ARE OUT OF WAR

Oct 3, Damascus General Allenby's troops have been fighting the Turks in Judaea and Palestine. They have now captured Damascus. Arab troops from the Hejaz have turned the Turks out of Arabia. They have also arrived at Damascus. The Arabs are led by Emir Feisal, son of the Sherif of Mecca, and an Englishman, Lt. Col. T. E. Lawrence. The Turks offered a reward of £20,000 for Lawrence, dead or alive. He led attacks on many Turkish troop trains. The Turks are now finally defeated.

T. E. Lawrence, painted by James McBey

RUSSIAN ROYAL FAMILY MURDERED

July 16, Siberia The ex-Tsar of Russia, his wife, three daughters and young son were shot dead today. They have been under house arrest in this remote part of the country. Their killers were the powerful Bolshevik security police, the Cheka.

Tsar Nicholas II of Russia with his son Alexis

AEROPLANES ARE HERE TO STAY

April 1, London   The Royal Flying Corps has today been renamed the Royal Air Force (RAF). The airforce has over 22,000 planes with British-made engines. In 1914 we had only 272, and the engines were made abroad. In those days airmen flew without parachutes. They had no chance of escape if their planes were shot down. Top speeds have increased too: from 80 mph in 1914 to 140 mph today. The Handley Page bomber can fly at an altitude of 7620 m (25,000 ft).

AN ARMISTICE IS SIGNED AT LAST

Nov 11, Forest of Compiègne, France   Four years of continuous fighting ended at 11 a.m. today. In France and Belgium, the two sides have fought over the same territory all this time. Now the guns are at last silent. Turkey and Austria are already out of the war. The German Kaiser has fled to Holland, and Germany has been declared a republic. Much of France and Belgium is in ruins.

Allied and German leaders signed the armistice agreement in a railway carriage.

One of the tasks facing Europe after the war is to erect lasting tributes to the fallen soldiers. These war graves are at Arras in France.

MATURE WOMEN VOTE IN PEACE-TIME ELECTION

Dec 28, London   Women over the age of 30 have been allowed to vote for the first time in a General Election. Suffragettes still want the voting age to be 21, as it is for men, but this is a step in the right direction. Mr. Lloyd George's government is back in office. The Prime Minister told voters he wanted to make Britain 'a land fit for heroes to live in'. Cries of 'Hang the Kaiser' and 'Make Germany pay' have been heard at election meetings. The main task of the new government will be to give jobs to returning soldiers, and to restore the economy which has been hard hit by war.

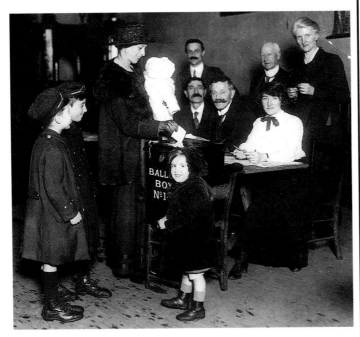

This woman, voting for the first time, has brought her young family with her.

NEW KILLER DISEASE DIAGNOSED

Oct 26, London   Schools and offices have closed because so many people have severe aches and pains, coughs and sneezes. An influenza epidemic has been raging all over the world. It is a serious form of the disease. Millions of people have died. India and China have been very badly hit. The United States lost half a million people in 10 months. More people are likely to die of influenza than were killed in four years of fighting during the war. There is no cure for the disease.

AMERICA GAINS WHILE EUROPE DECLINES

Dec, New York   America has come out of the war without the ruin that faces other countries. Business has boomed, and factories have been working round the clock. The USA is now in a very favourable position, and may very well become the leading nation of the world.

POET WHO DENIED THAT WAR IS 'GLORIOUS'

Nov 4, France   The English poet, Wilfred Owen, has been killed in action. Many hundreds of young men were taught at home and at school that death in battle was valiant and noble. They learnt a Latin phrase which means 'It is sweet and fitting to die for one's country.' In one poem, Owen called this 'the old lie'. His poetry reflects war's stupidity and waste. He died just as the war was ending.

NEWS IN BRIEF . . .

MUSIC JOINED THE WAR EFFORT

Nov 30, New York   While America was at war, the city's orchestra refused to play music by living German composers. Many Americans extended this ban to all German composers. They refused to listen to music by Beethoven, Brahms or Mozart.

SCHOOL WILL LAST ANOTHER YEAR

March 13, London   If a new Bill is passed in parliament, children will in future have to stay at school until they are 14. After that the government wants them to attend part-time courses until they are 18. This means that youngsters will not be competing for jobs with returning soldiers. The extra year should also raise the standard of education all over the country.

RATIONING MEANS FAIR SHARES FOR ALL

March, London   Some foods are being rationed. Ration books containing coupons are being printed. The coupons will be exchanged for food. These are the amounts one person is allowed each week:

Sugar	227g (8oz)
Butter/margarine	142g (5oz)
Meat	450g (16oz)
Jam	113g (4oz)
Tea	57g (2oz)

1919

PEACE PROPOSALS IN PARIS
PRESIDENT SUGGESTS LEAGUE OF WORLD NATIONS

Feb 14, Paris In the Palace of Versailles, delegates from 51 nations are working out the Peace Treaty. All these nations want to avoid war in the future. It is difficult to decide how this can be done. US President Woodrow Wilson has suggested that they should form a council called the 'League of Nations'. He would like America to belong to it.

GERMANS MUST PAY FOR THE WAR

May 7, Paris The Peace Treaty has finally been agreed on, after much discussion. President Wilson wanted Europeans to forget the war and start afresh. The French, who have to rebuild their towns and villages, want Germany to pay heavily. The Treaty they have drawn up says that Germany started the war, and must pay 'reparations' of about £6600 million to the Allies, and must reduce her army and weapons. The conference agreed that a League of Nations should be set up.

GERMANS DISAGREE WITH PEACE PROPOSALS

May 31, Paris The German Chancellor has resigned rather than sign the Peace Treaty. The Germans say they took no part in drawing it up. They do not agree that they were the only country responsible for the war. They are also shocked at the size of the reparations. But the Allies will not back down.

POLAND HAS A CORRIDOR TO DANZIG

June 28, Warsaw Poland has been part of Russia for 50 years. A clause in the Peace Treaty has made her an independent country. She has been given a strip of land crossing German territory. This will give her an outlet to the Baltic Sea. She will be able to use the port of Danzig. Danzig, once German, has been made a 'free city' by the Treaty of Versailles.

GERMAN FLEET SUNK

June 21, Scapa Flow, Scotland German prisoners-of-war sank seventy of their own ships in Scapa Flow harbour today. The Allies are shocked at this action. The ships were docked at this remote port while the Peace Conference decided what to do with them. The German Admiral says he was obeying an order never to surrender his warships.

German sailors arrive on shore after scuttling their ship at Scapa Flow.

PEACE TREATY SIGNED IN SILENCE

June 28, Paris   This afternoon two German representatives came to the Palace of Versailles. They entered the Hall of Mirrors, where the Presidents of the United States and France, and the Prime Ministers of Great Britain and Italy, sat in silence. The Germans signed the Peace Treaty. Without speaking, they walked out of the Hall. The German nation feels it has been forced into accepting terms which are unreasonable.

The silent German delegation at Versailles

GERMAN UNREST LEADS TO UPRISING

Jan 15, Berlin   The murder in custody of Rosa Luxembourg and Karl Liebnecht has shocked Germany. They were leaders of a Communist group called the 'Sparticists'. In Germany's confused state, political parties with violent aims are being formed. The Sparticists tried to start a revolution. Another new group, the Frei Korps, is being blamed for the murders. Though they helped the government troops defeat the Sparticists, they also threaten Germany's future.

INNOCENT BYSTANDERS MASSACRED AT AMRITSAR

April 13, Amritsar, India   Thousands of people were gathered together today in a public walled garden in the city. Many were in Amritsar as pilgrims to the holy Sikh temple. Others had gone to listen to Indian speakers protest about new British government laws. Last week public meetings were banned because of serious rioting in Amritsar. General Dyer, who commands British and Indian troops, heard about the gathering. He marched 50 Gurkha soldiers into the garden and ordered them to fire on the crowd. They fired for 10 minutes. Most of the Indians were killed; many were young children. This brutal attack will make Indians more determined to break away from the British Empire.

ANTI-GOVERNMENT PROTEST IN CHINA

Nov 4, Peking, China   By the Peace Treaty, Japan was given a part of Shantung province, which was once German territory. The Chinese government accepted this decision. But on May 4, three thousand students from the new Peking University demonstrated against it in Tian-an-men Square. The demonstration was peaceful until someone attacked a pro-Japanese official. Then government troops arrested over 1000 young men and women. Students in 200 towns also demonstrated against the government. The public supported the students: shops closed, and factories went on strike. The government has been forced to release the jailed students.

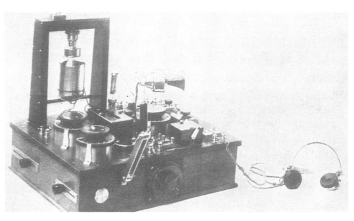
In March, Marconi used this wireless telephone to transmit signals from Ireland to Nova Scotia.

1919

HERO HOLDS PORT

Sept 23, Italy Signor Gabriele D'Annunzio, with 2000 men, has occupied Fiume. Fiume used to be part of the Austrian Empire, but it has a large Italian population. Earlier this year it became a 'free' port under League of Nations protection. Signor D'Annunzio has popular support, but not the approval of the Italian government.

THE FASCISTS ARE A GROWING PARTY

Oct 31, Milan Benito Mussolini, an Italian journalist, founded a new political party called the Fascists last March. After only seven months it has a membership of 17,000. The Fascists want many reforms. These include more land for the peasants, pensions, and an eight-hour day in factories. The Fascist party appeals to many Italians.

NEWS IN BRIEF . . .

TRIUMPH FOR AMERICAN WOMEN

June 4, Washington The Federal Constitution of America has been amended. In future, no citizen of the United States will be denied the right to vote because of their sex. The suffragettes have won their fight for the right to vote.

BOXER'S WIN IS A WALK-OVER

July 4, Toledo, Ohio Jack Dempsey has become the world heavyweight boxing champion. He defeated Jess Willard so heavily that spectators called for the fight to be stopped. The huge Jess Willard seemed astonished at Dempsey's power. He is unlikely to continue boxing.

STYLISH WIMBLEDON

July 5, Wimbledon France's 20-year-old Suzanne Lenglen has beaten the British champion Dorothea Chambers. It was also a meeting of old and new styles of dress. Miss Chambers wore the usual ankle-length dress with long sleeves. By comparison, Miss Lenglen looked freer and cooler in a short-sleeved blouse and calf-length skirt.

NANCY ASTOR IS FIRST WOMAN MP

Dec 1, London Lady Nancy Astor today took her seat in the House of Commons. She was elected as MP for Plymouth. This is a historic occasion, and one the suffragettes fought for. Nancy Astor is encouraging other women to stand for parliament.

Lady Nancy Astor, MP

FIVE COUNTRIES HAVE LOST THEIR HEADS

Dec 30 Since 1910, five countries have decided not to be ruled by a king or emperor. Instead, they will have an elected leader. Portugal, China, Russia, Austria and Germany were all monarchies or empires ten years ago, and now they are all republics.

RELATIVITIY IS RIGHT

March 29, London 'The greatest genius on earth' is how Albert Einstein is now described. Members of the Royal Society of London took photographs of a total eclipse of the sun. They made many calculations, based on the photographs. These show that Einstein's Theory of Relativity is correct.

Albert Einstein, the physicist

PEOPLE OF THE NINETEEN-TENS

David Lloyd George, British politician 1863 – 1945

Lloyd George entered Parliament as a Liberal in 1890. He was Chancellor of the Exchequer from 1908 to 1915. He became Prime Minister in 1916, but his party was defeated in 1922. Lloyd George was a charming man, and a witty debater. He came from a poor background, and fought for social reform, introducing health and unemployment benefits in 1911. He sympathized with the Irish, and started the talks that led to the Government of Ireland Act of 1920. Just before he died he became Earl Lloyd-George of Dwyfor.

Jan Christiaan Smuts, South African leader 1870 – 1950

Smuts fought against the British in the Boer War of 1899. He was a very daring guerrilla fighter. He became pro-British when the Labour Government granted self-government to South Africa in 1909. During the Great War his forces attacked German colonies in East Africa. In 1917 he became a member of the Allied War Cabinet. He helped to create the RAF. In 1919 he became Prime Minister of South Africa. He opposed apartheid, but was not able to stop it. He welcomed the League of Nations in 1919, and the United Nations Organization in 1945.

Vladimir Ilyich Lenin 1870 – 1924

Lenin was the leader of the Bolsheviks in Russia. He was a well-educated and intelligent man. Lenin became a revolutionary when his brother was hanged in 1887 (he had been in a plot to kill Tsar Alexander). Lenin spent his youth dodging the police, or in exile. He hoped the Great War would end capitalism. Then the workers of the world might rule their own countries.

In Russia in 1917 he seized his chance. Over the next five years he became a dictator and crushed other political parties, bringing Communism to the whole Russian empire. In his last years he regretted the path Bolshevism was taking. He thought the rule of Josef Stalin would be bad for the country. He died in 1924 after suffering two strokes.

Woodrow Wilson, American politician 1856 – 1924

Wilson was elected President of the United States in 1912, and he held this position until 1920. He tried to keep America out of World War I. But when the Germans continued to attack American ships, and particularly the civilian *Lusitania*, he finally asked the Senate to declare war in 1917. After the war, Wilson was a leading figure at the Peace Conference. The League of Nations was his idea. Although he urged the American Senate to join the League, they refused to do so. Wilson fell ill in 1919. He retired from politics a disappointed man.

Sarah Bernhardt, French actress 1844 – 1923

Sarah Bernhardt's American debut in 1880 was so popular that tickets were being sold on the black market. Audiences loved this petite brunette with the golden voice. She continued to play the role of young women into her 50s with great success. In 1912 she starred in two French films: *Queen Elizabeth* and *The Lady of the Camellias*. Two years later she had to have a leg amputated, but she continued to act. The French government made her a member of the Legion of Honour.

Erich von Ludendorff, German general 1865 – 1937

General von Ludendorff took part in the first march into Belgium in 1914. He was transferred to the Eastern Front. He defeated General Samsonov at the Battle of Tannenburg. His strategy caused the defeat of the Serbians, and the Italians at Caporetto. The Hindenburg Line was his idea. He agreed that the Germans should sink ships of all nations.

In 1917 he helped Lenin return to Russia from Switzerland. He put him on a special sealed train through Germany. He hoped that a Russian revolution would help the German war effort. The following year he planned the last great German offensive. When it failed, he asked the Kaiser to make peace. He was dismissed on October 26. For a time in the 1920s and 1930s he backed Hitler. But after a lifetime of war, von Ludendorff became a pacifist in his last years.

Isadora Duncan, American dancer 1878 – 1927

Isadora Duncan based her dancing on the figures painted on Greek vases. She shocked people in many countries because of her see-through clothing and bare feet. Once the Berlin police banned her performance, saying it was obscene.

Americans were scandalized by her private life. She had many lovers, and two illegitimate children. Both children were drowned in an accident in 1913. In 1921 she was invited to Moscow, and Lenin gave her a house to live in. She taught dancing there, and married a Russian poet. He was mentally ill, and in 1925 he hanged himself. Isadora died in a freak accident in France. She was in an open car when her long red scarf caught in the spoked wheel. As the car sped on, the scarf strangled her.

For the first time ever

1910	UK	First public escalator opened
		First woman professor appointed
		First woman officer joins police force
	USA	First model aeroplane kits on sale
		First domestic refrigerator on sale
	France	Neon tube lighting invented
1911	Germany	Windscreen wipers invented
	UK	First nursery school opened
	USA	First film studio opened, in Hollywood
		White lines painted down the middle of the road
	India	First airmail service
1912	New Zealand	Widows get pensions
	Germany	Zips first used in clothing
	USA	Airman parachuted from his plane
	France	Neon tubing used in advertising
1913	USA	First crosswords in a newspaper
		Brillo pads invented
		First woman magistrate appointed
	France	Cellophane manufactured
	UK	First stainless steel knives
		Tanks developed secretly
		Dry shaver on the market
		Police officers carry electric torches instead of oil-lamps
1914	UK	Photos necessary on passports
		First Cub pack is formed
	USA	Traffic lights first powered by electricity
		Mothers' Day celebrated (May 9)
	USSR	Russian plane serves first in-flight meals
	Germany	Tear gas produced
1915	Germany	First all-metal aeroplane
	UK	Tanks first used in battle
		The Women's Institute formed
		First Brownie pack formed
	USA	Pyrex glass ovenware on sale
		First taxis on New York streets

1916	UK	Britain changes to Summer Time
		First electric lawn mower
	USA	Liquid nail polish on sale
1917	USA	First recording made, of the Dixieland Jazz Band
		First birth-control clinic opened
	UK	Londoners hear first air raid sirens
	Italy	Special airmail stamps
1918	USA	First pop-up toasters on sale
		First electric-powered clock
1919	USA	First radio broadcast
		First science fiction magazine
	UK	First wall plugs, Rawlplugs, on sale

New words and expressions

New inventions, and new habits or occupations, cause people to invent new words. They also invent new slang. These are some of the words and phrases used for the first time between 1910 and 1919 in England and America.

aerofoil	get-together
alibi	give something a miss
allergy	hangover
Anzac	I.Q. (intelligence
blotto	quotient)
collage	it's a cinch
come to a sticky end	it's a good buy
conk out	joyride
out for the count	kite (plane)
crush (crowd)	lowbrow
digs	lunatic fringe
dog-fight	Mills bomb
draft	on the wagon
ersatz	radio
fibrositis	roneo
flame-thrower	stand in a queue
flashback	slipstream
flop	tempo
fly-past	that's her all over
geneticist	well, what d'you know?

How many of these words and expressions do we still use today? Do you know what they all mean?

Glossary

amendment: a change or addition to a document.

armistice: agreement to stop a war.

Bolsheviks: Russian political party. They believed in rule by the people, not by a Tsar. They are the original Communist Party.

chassis: the frame of a motor vehicle (pronounced 'shassy').

concerto: music for a solo instrument, accompanied by an orchestra.

coup: an illegal change of government. Short for *coup d'état*, which means 'a blow at the state'.

covenant: a contract, or agreement.

cubist painting: style of art where straight lines and cubes are used to represent curves and circles.

dominion: a self-governing territory of the British Commonwealth.

dynasty: a family of rulers.

Fascists: Italian political party, anti-Communist. Its leader, Benito Mussolini, ruled Italy as a dictator. The name comes from Latin. *Fasces* (bundles of rods) were carried in front of the Roman Emperor as a sign of his authority.

free city: a city which rules itself, and does not belong to any one nation.

gunboat: a small armed ship.

influenza: a virus disease. Sufferers have fever and aching limbs.

Ku Klux Klan: a secret racist society of whites formed in the southern states of America after the Civil War.

milliner: a person who makes hats.

Morse code: an alphabet invented by Samuel Morse to send messages. Each letter has its own combination of dots and dashes.

no man's land: territory between opposing sides in a war, claimed by neither.

outcaste: a Hindu who does not belong to any caste. Outcastes are regarded as unfit for any but the most unpleasant jobs.

parole: word of honour. A prisoner on parole is allowed to live at home; he gives his word not to escape.

picket: people who stand outside a workplace to persuade others to join a strike.

posthumous: after death.

radium: a radioactive metal.

reparations: compensation for war damage.

Sikh: a member of an Indian religious group.

spats: a short cover for men's shoes. Spats were made of cloth and fastened under the shoe with a strap.

suffragettes: women who campaigned for the vote (suffrage).

treason: illegal plotting against the monarch or government.

whaling station: a permanent base for whale-hunting.

Further Reading

The Twentieth Century World: Peter and Mary Speed. Oxford University Press 1982

Great Lives of the Twentieth Century: Ed. Alan Bullock. Weidenfeld 1981

A History of the Twentieth Century: D. B. O'Callaghan. Longman 1987

Picture History of the 20th Century series; *1900–19*: Richard Tames. Franklin Watts 1991

How We Used to Live 1902–26: Freda Kelsall. A & C Black 1987

The Twentieth Century: R J Unstead. A & C Black 1974

How and Why: Russian Revolution: Elizabeth Campling. Batsford

Portrait of a Decade series; *1910–1919*: Trevor Fisher. Batsford

The First World War: John Pimlott. Franklin Watts

How they Lived series; *A Soldier in World War I*: Wayland 1987

World War One: Robert Hoare. Macdonald Educational 1985